· FUN · WITH · MATH ·

MEASURING

LAKSHMI HEWAVISENTI

Gloucester Press
New York · London · Toronto · Sydney

© Aladdin Books Ltd 1991

Design: David West
Children's Book Design
Editor: Melanie Halton
Illustrators: John Kelly
Ian Moores

*First published in the United States
in 1991 by*
Gloucester Press
387 Park Avenue South
New York, NY 10016

Library of Congress Cataloging-
in-Publication Data

Hewavisenti, Lakshmi.
Measuring / by Lakshmi
Hewavisenti.
p.   cm. -- (Fun with math)
Includes index.
Summary: Presents activities
involving quantity, proportion,
length and weight, estimating and
approximating with numbers, and
graphic representation.
ISBN 0-531-17319-4
1. Mensuration--Juvenile literature.
(1. Arithmetic. 2. Measurement.) I.
Title. II. Series.
QA465.H49   1991
530.8--dc20
91-10767   CIP   AC

Printed in Belgium

CONTENTS

INTRODUCTION

Is the distance around your hand longer than your arm? Which of your friends can run the fastest? You'll learn how to find these answers in this book – and try many other measuring activities that are enjoyable to do. Learning how to measure can be really fun – and you can learn a lot of new things at the same time!

VOLUME

If an apple were hollow, would it hold more water than a cup? There is a way to find out which one has more volume (holds more) – try this experiment with other objects, too.

Measuring volume
Put the apple in the measuring glass and cover it with water. Write down the number that the water reaches on the glass. Now remove the apple and take down the new number. Subtract to find the volume of the apple.

What you need

Measuring glass

Mixing bowl

Plastic bottle

Baking tray

Egg

Stone

Apple

Pencil

Ruler

Tomato

Paper

Hand volume
Use the same method to measure the volume of other things, including your hand. Try it for bigger hands, too!

Make a graph

Guess and measure the volumes of the other objects. Then draw a chart like this one to show your results.

FLUID OUNCES

8
7
6
5
4
3
2
1

BALL EGG STONE APPLE TOMATO POTATO

OBJECT

Guessing the volume

Guess the volumes of each container. Now fill them with water. Empty each one into the measuring glass and check the numbers to see if your guesses were right.

Bowl

Washing liquid bottle with top cut off

Egg cup

Pour water into each of the containers.

Baking tray

SIZE & WEIGHT

If two objects have the same weight, do you think they have to have the same size? Here is an experiment you can do to see if you are right.

What to do
To start with, weigh out three equal balls of modeling clay. Make sure they weigh exactly the same amount. Now mold them into three different shapes.

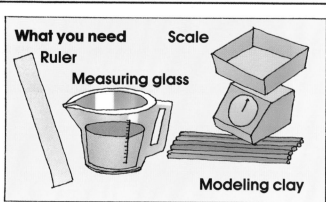

What you need   Scale
Ruler
Measuring glass
Modeling clay

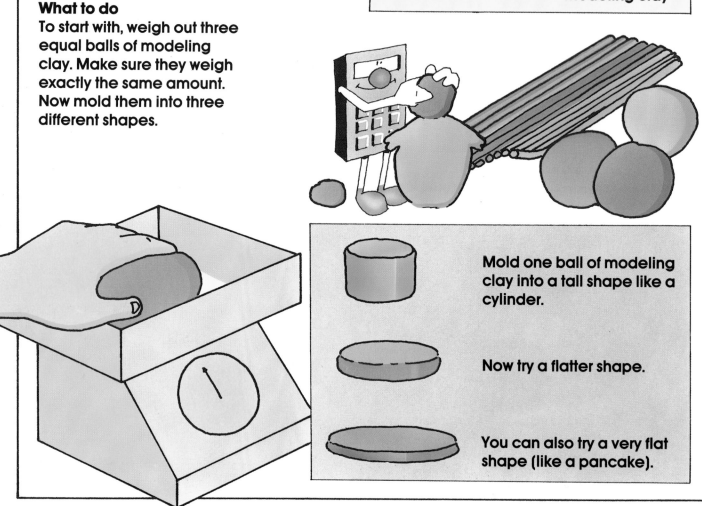

Mold one ball of modeling clay into a tall shape like a cylinder.

Now try a flatter shape.

You can also try a very flat shape (like a pancake).

Estimating volume

Try putting your three shapes into a measuring glass of water. Make sure the water covers your shape without spilling out. Does the water level go up to the same mark for all three shapes?

Hollow out and weigh

Now try making two shapes of about the same size. Make one of them hollow. Which one weighs more?

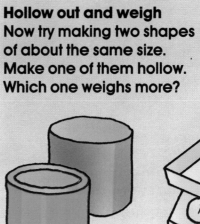

The same volume?

Using your three equal pieces of modeling clay, make the thick, medium and thin shapes shown here. Check their volumes — did you think they would be the same?

TEMPERATURE

These are activities that will give you an idea of how long water takes to get cold...or turn to ice.

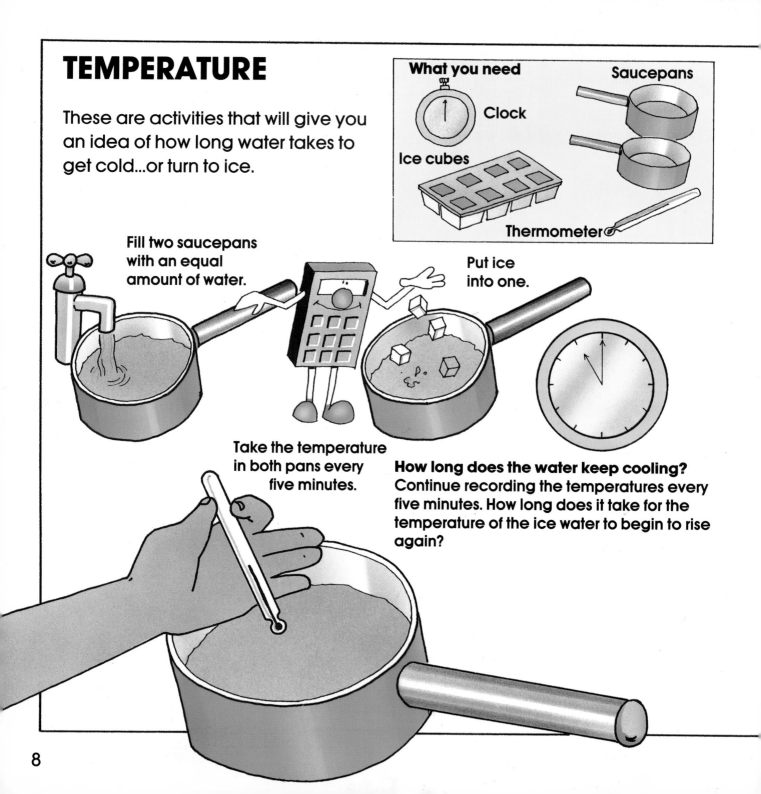

What you need

Clock

Saucepans

Ice cubes

Thermometer

Fill two saucepans with an equal amount of water.

Put ice into one.

Take the temperature in both pans every five minutes.

How long does the water keep cooling?
Continue recording the temperatures every five minutes. How long does it take for the temperature of the ice water to begin to rise again?

How fast will water freeze?

For this experiment, you will need two plastic cups. Put some water into each one, and add some salt to one of them. Make sure that both the cups have about the same amount of water in them.

Put both containers in the freezer. Guess which one will freeze first, and keep checking every 30 minutes or so. Then, when you see signs of the water freezing, check them every five minutes.

Did they both freeze?
Which one froze more quickly?
What does salt do?

Were you right?
How long did it take?

9

SPEED

Speed is another way of saying "how fast." So your running speed is higher than your walking speed. This activity shows you how you can measure your speed.

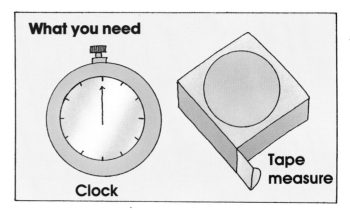

What you need

Clock

Tape measure

What to do
Mark a starting line. Ask a friend to start the clock and shout "Go." When you hear this, run as fast as you can.

After ten seconds, your friend should shout "Stop." Mark the point you have reached. Now measure the distance you ran.

If you could keep running at this speed, you could run double this distance in 20 seconds. So if you run 20 yards in 10 seconds, your distance in 20 seconds would be twice as far — 40 yards.

10 SECONDS

20 YARDS

Try this
If you pretend that you can keep running at the same speed indefinitely, you can figure out how far you could run in any time period.

30 SECS
3 × 20
= 60 YARDS

How many yards per minute?
There are 60 seconds in a minute, so to find your distance per minute, multiply six times the distance you ran in ten seconds.

1 MINUTE
6 × 20
= 120 YARDS

How many yards per hour?
There are 60 minutes in an hour. Multiply your last answer by 60 to find out how far you can run in an hour (... × 60 =... yards per hour). You can time your friends in the same way (and figure out their speeds), or see what your speeds are when you hop or skip for ten seconds.

120 YARDS
× 60
7200 YARDS
PER HOUR

TIME AND DISTANCE

This activity is a little like the one you did for speed (pg.10-11), but slightly different – this time you stop when you are ready, and not when your friend tells you to!

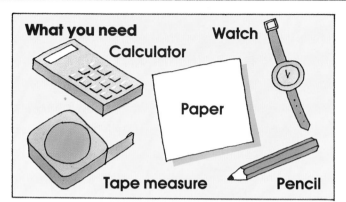

What you need

Calculator

Watch

Paper

Tape measure

Pencil

Use a tape measure to mark out a distance of 30 yards. Get your friend to time how long you take to walk to the other end.

30 yards

Let's say you took ten seconds. How far had you walked in half the time (five seconds)? In one second? How long would it take you to walk 60 yards? 120 yards?

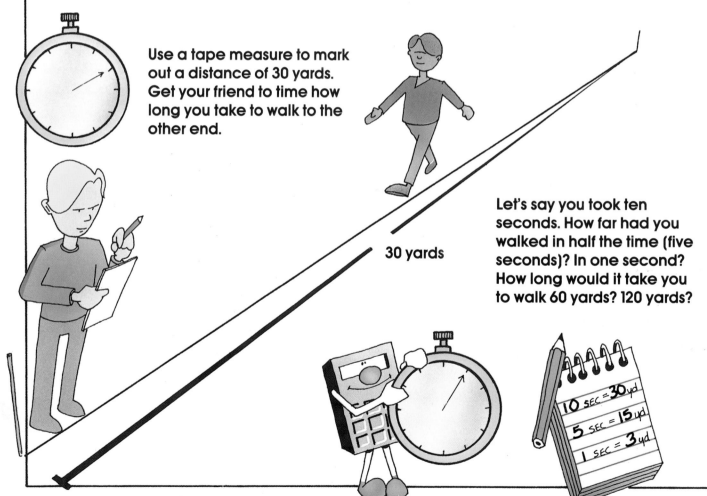

10 SEC = 30 yd
5 SEC = 15 yd
1 SEC = 3 yd

Time yourself taking a bath

Bath times can give you a lot of information, too! Time how long it takes to fill up the tub. After your bath, decide if the tub will empty in the same time as it took to fill up. Check by letting the water out!

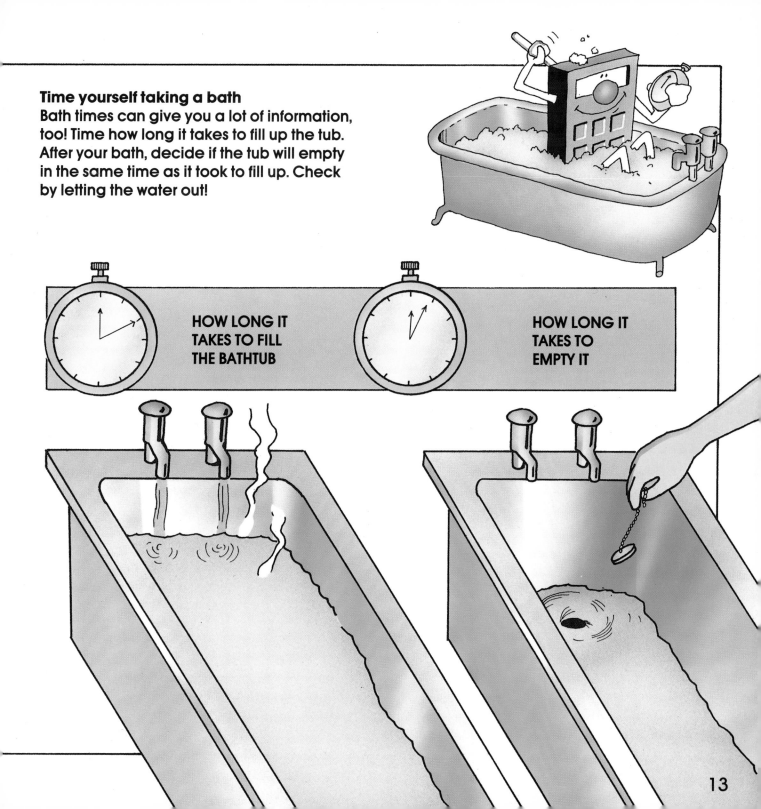

HOW LONG IT TAKES TO FILL THE BATHTUB

HOW LONG IT TAKES TO EMPTY IT

JUDGING DISTANCE

What can you use to help you guess distances? It depends on whether you want to measure a short, medium or long distance. Try these ideas.

Medium distance
Find a sidewalk with several parked cars. Use the cars to help you to judge distance. Measure the first car and use this as a guide for the lengths of the others.

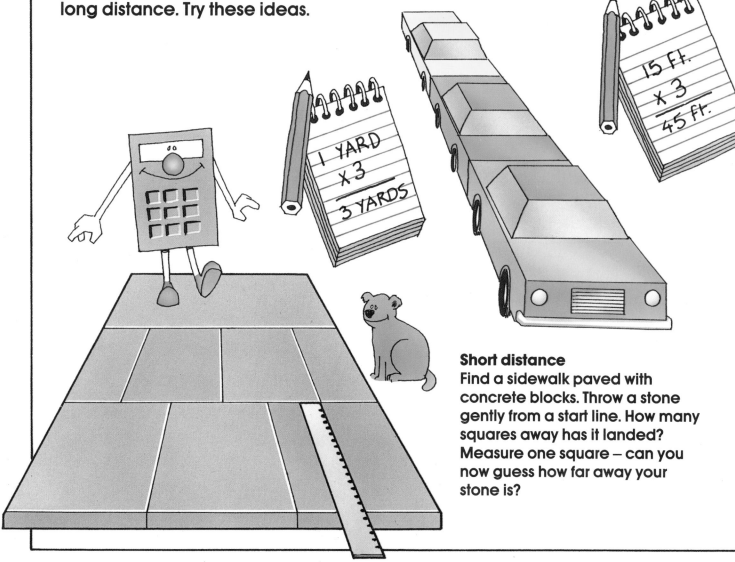

Short distance
Find a sidewalk paved with concrete blocks. Throw a stone gently from a start line. How many squares away has it landed? Measure one square – can you now guess how far away your stone is?

Long distance

You can use a similar method to this in order to judge longer distances – streetlights, houses or telephone poles will help you here.

Far away

You can even have a rough guess at the distance to the top of a tall building. Measure the distance from the ground to the top of the first row of windows. Now count how many rows you see and multiply that figure times your measurement.

LENGTH & DISTANCE

Sometimes rulers are not the best tools to use for measuring. Tape measures are useful for long distances, and string is good for things that are not straight.

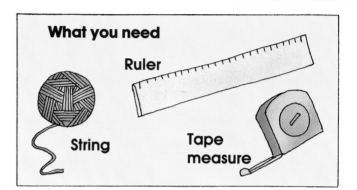

What you need

Ruler

String

Tape measure

Measure distance
Make a mark from here, and gently throw a ball. Guess how far away it lands. Now use a tape measure to find the distance. Was your guess right?

Measuring with string

You can measure the distance around your hand with a piece of string that is long enough. Use a ruler (or tape measure) to see how much string was used.

Try this

To find the distance around the outline of your body, lie down and get some friends to fit the string around you!

The length of your foot

Mark off the ends of your foot on a piece of paper. Measure this with a ruler. Try a bigger person's foot, and a smaller foot, too, if there is one!

WAYS OF MEASURING

Before people invented rulers, they used other objects for measuring. Parts of the body were often used, and even today people use "paces" or "hands" to measure some things.

What you need

String

Pencils

Spaghetti noodles

What to do
See how much string you need to go around your head. Measure the string with a ruler. Try measuring other round things. Use spaghetti noodles to measure straight things, like your table or bed. Measure your room in "paces."

Try this
You can use a pencil to help you measure things. How many pencils high is a table?

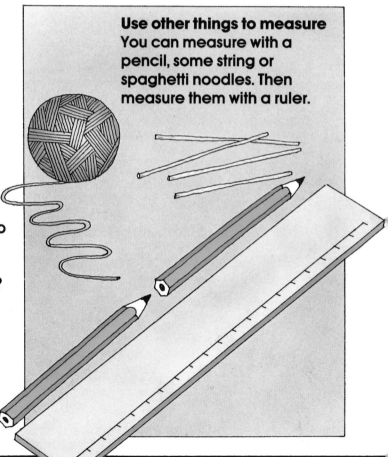

Use other things to measure
You can measure with a pencil, some string or spaghetti noodles. Then measure them with a ruler.

MEASURING WITH YOUR BODY

Arm span
The arm span from the spine to the tip of the middle finger is roughly two cubits (see right) and is also half of a person's height.

Cubit

Hand
A hand is from the wrist to the tip of the middle finger.

Hand span
Your hand span is from the tip of the thumb to the little finger.

Measuring a horse
The height of a horse is measured in "hands." One hand equals four inches.

Cubit
The measurement from your elbow to the tip of your middle finger is known as a cubit. Cubits were used in measuring thousands of years ago.

Foot pace
Measure the distance of one of your footsteps. This gives you the length of a foot pace.

AREA

To compare and measure the area (the size of the surface) of different shapes, draw them onto graph paper and then count the squares.

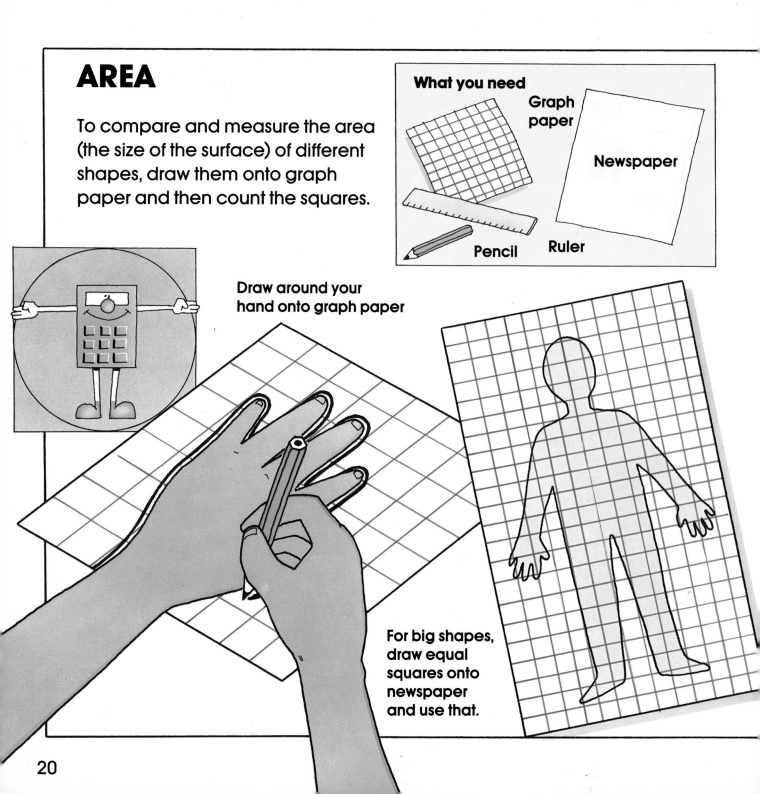

What you need

Graph paper

Newspaper

Pencil   Ruler

Draw around your hand onto graph paper

For big shapes, draw equal squares onto newspaper and use that.

Measure your bedroom
You can make an accurate drawing of your bedroom using graph paper. First, measure your room and the furniture. Now draw it all in position. Each 1cm square of the paper could represent, say, 15cm.

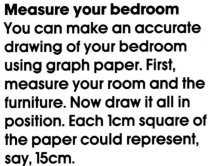

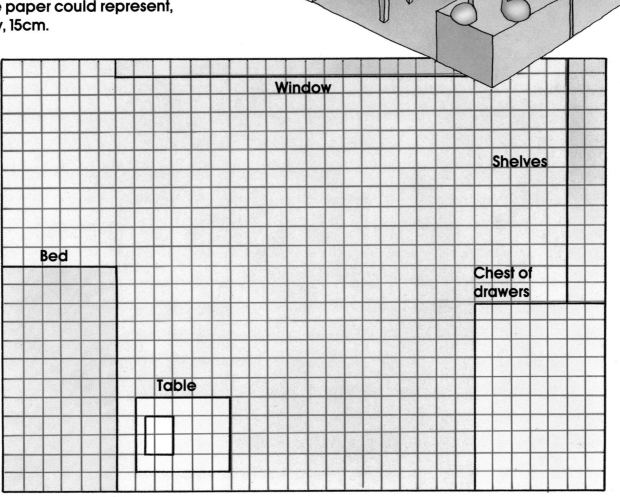

Window

Shelves

Bed

Chest of drawers

Table

WEIGHING

Can you always tell which is the heavier of two things just by holding them or looking at them? In this activity you check weights to see how close your guesses were.

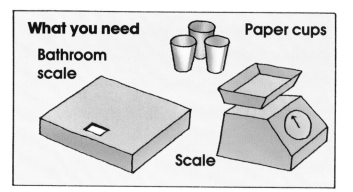

What you need

Bathroom scale

Paper cups

Scale

Estimating weight
First find several objects like these and put them in a line from lightest to heaviest (guess the order by feeling and comparing the objects). Now check by using a scale.

Size and weight

Does a cup of rice weigh the same as a cup of flour? Try filling some paper cups with different things like salt, peas, peanuts, and so on. Guess the order from the lightest to the heaviest. Check each one with the scale. Were you right?

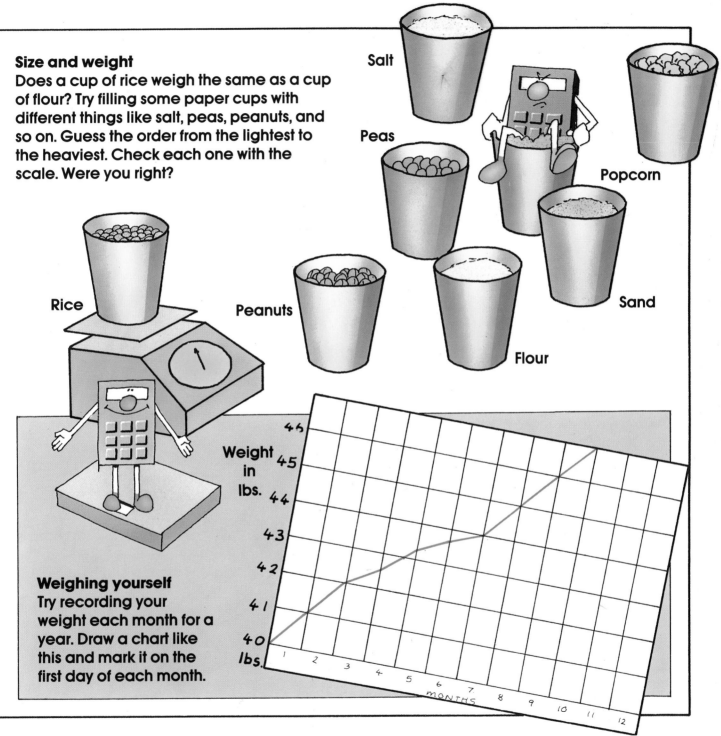

Salt

Peas

Popcorn

Rice

Peanuts

Flour

Sand

Weighing yourself
Try recording your weight each month for a year. Draw a chart like this and mark it on the first day of each month.

Weight in lbs.

46
45
44
43
42
41
40
lbs.

1 2 3 4 5 6 7 8 9 10 11 12
MONTHS

STRAW SCALE

Have you ever thought about making your own scale to compare the weight of small things like paperclips, peas and matchsticks? Here is how you can make a straw scale.

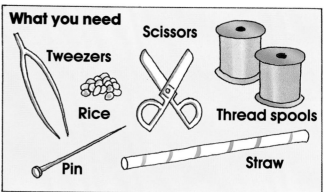

What you need

Tweezers

Rice

Scissors

Thread spools

Pin

Straw

First step
Cut out a scoop at both ends of the straw. Make sure they match in size.

How to make the scale
Push a pin through the middle of the straw and balance it on two thread spools, as below. If it doesn't balance, put a small paper "rider," or loop, on the higher side, and move it around until you get a perfect balance.

Things to measure
Now try weighing something small, like a
peanut, by putting it into one of the scoops.
Balance your scale by using grains of rice on
the other side. You will need to be gentle
and use tweezers. Make a note of how many
rice grains you use. Weigh other objects in
the same way.

Try this
You can compare the
weights of bigger
objects by using a large
cardboard tube instead
of a straw.

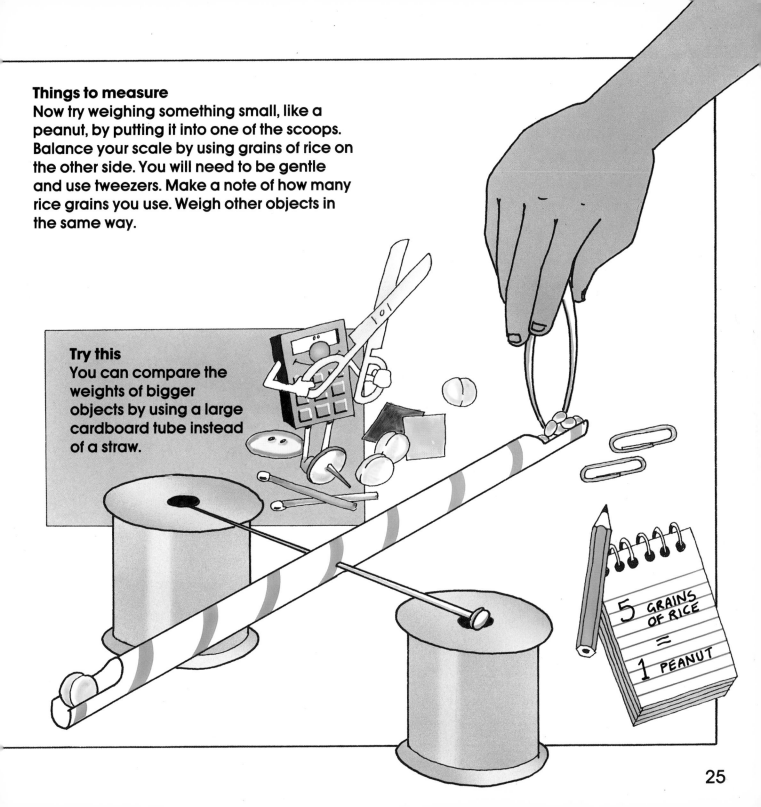

5 GRAINS
OF RICE
=
1 PEANUT

WEIGHING-RULER

This is an experiment that will help you compare the weights of different objects without using a weighing scale. Instead you will use a weighing-ruler.

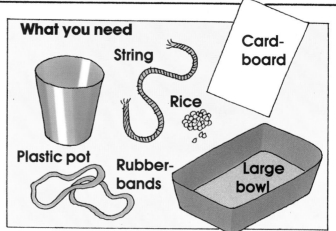

What you need
String
Card-board
Rice
Plastic pot
Rubber-bands
Large bowl

How to make it
Put the string through the rubberband and tie it onto the pot. Now hang this on a door handle and put the bowl under it.

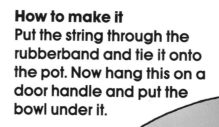

Put the cardboard behind the pot as the picture shows. Mark the cardboard where the top of the empty pot reaches.

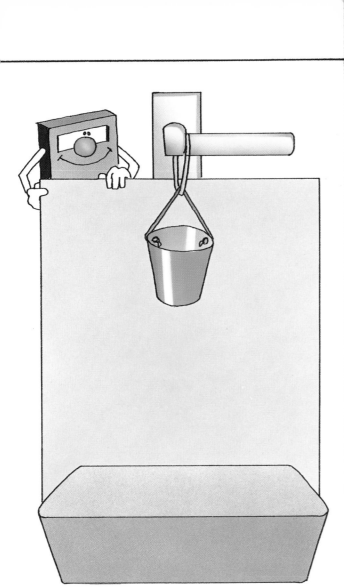

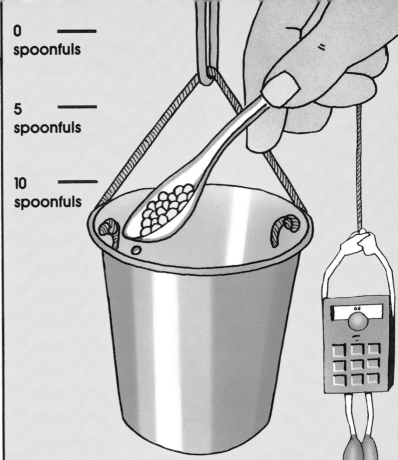

Using your chart

Use this weighing-ruler to weigh other objects. If your rubberband has stretched, you will need to start again with a new one of the same size as the original rubberband.

Measuring rice in cups

Now you are ready to start the experiment. Gently add five spoonfuls of rice into the pot. Mark where the top of the pot reaches now. Keep adding the rice, five spoonfuls at a time, and keep marking the cardboard as you go along. You can also try weighing other objects, like marbles or small candies. Keep a record of their weights on the same piece of cardboard and compare them.

SPEEDY SEEDS

How fast does a plant grow? Try growing plants from seeds and take measurements each day. To make it interesting, try growing one in the dark and one in the light.

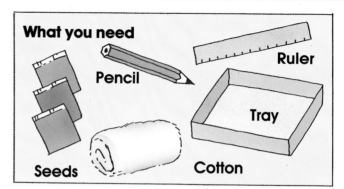

What you need

Pencil

Ruler

Tray

Seeds

Cotton

Growing mustard seeds
First, put a layer of cotton in a plastic tray or box. Dampen the cotton with water. Sprinkle the mustard seeds on top.

Recording growth
After two or three days you will see the shoots. Measure them each day. When did they grow most quickly? When did they stop growing?

Comparing growth

Follow the same steps again, but this time divide your tray in half. Sprinkle one half with mustard seeds and the other half with alfalfa seeds. Keep a chart of their daily heights. Which grew faster?

Try this

Use two trays and sprinkle each with one kind of seed. Cover one and put the other in a light place. Which one do you think will grow faster?

WEIGHTS & MEASURES

Here is a list of measuring terms and mathematical symbols that you will find helpful. As you do more math, this information will come in handy!

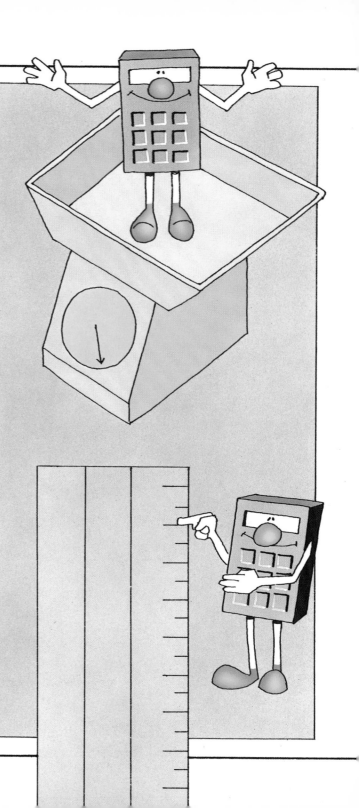

ABBREVIATIONS

g = gram	oz = ounce
kg= kilogram	lb = pound
mm = millimeter	in = inch
cm = centimeter	ft = foot
m = meter	yd = yard
km = kilometer	mi = mile
ml = milliliter	fl oz = fluid ounce
l = liter	pt = pint

WEIGHT

1,000g = 1kg	16oz = 1lb
1kg	2lb 3oz

LENGTH/DISTANCE

10mm = 1cm	12in = 1ft
100cm = 1m	36in = 1yd
1,000mm = 1m	3ft = 1yd
1,000m = 1km	5,280ft = 1mi
1km	⅗mi = 3,279ft

VOLUME

1,000ml = 1l	16fl oz = 1 pt

TIME

60 seconds	=	1 minute
15 minutes	=	¼ hour
30 minutes	=	½ hour
60 minutes	=	1 hour
24 hours	=	1 day
365 days	=	1 year

ABBREVIATIONS

sec	=	second
min	=	minute
hr	=	hour
yr	=	year

ARITHMETIC SIGNS

+ ADDITION (plus)

— SUBTRACTION (minus)

✕ MULTIPLICATION (multiply by)

÷ DIVISION (divide by)

= EQUALITY (equals)

INDEX

ANSWERS

Page 9: Salt water freezes more slowly.

Page 12: If you took 10 secs to walk 30yds., in 5 secs. you walked 15yds.; in one sec. you walked 3yds. To walk 60yds. you would take 20 secs.; 120yds. would take 40 secs.

PRINTED IN BELGIUM BY
proos
INTERNATIONAL BOOK PROD